Contents

Levels*	Instrumentation†	Title	Composer	Page
B B	tpt hn	Soccarocca	John Miller	2
B B	tpt hn	Wonky Waltz	Nick Breeze	3
B B	tpt LB	Megamarch	James Rae	4
B B	tpt LB	Passing Through	Chris Batchelor	5
B B	hn LB	Two for Tea (i)	Philip Harper	6
		Two for Tea (ii)		7
B B	hn LB	Bought me a cat (i)	Trad. American	8
		Bought me a cat (ii)	arr. Paul Archibald	9
B B B	tpt tpt hn	Alpine Echo	Ian Lowes	10
B B B	tpt tpt LB	Dancing Bears	Adrian Taylor	12
B B B	tpt tpt LB	Promenade	Kit Turnbull	13
B B S	hn LB LB	Tango para Tres (i)	Phil Croydon	14
		Tango para Tres (ii)		15
B S S	tpt hn LB	Russian Nights (i)	Philip Sparke	16
		Russian Nights (ii)		17
B S S	tpt hn LB	Ye Kinge (i)	David Mitcham	18
		Ye Kinge (ii)		20
B S S	tpt hn LB	Country Dance (i)	Trad. arr. Paul Archibald	22
		Country Dance (ii)		23
B C C C	tpt tpt LB LB	March	Susato arr. Paul Archibald	24
B B B B	tpt tpt hn LB	Last Chance	Nick Breeze	26
B B B S	hn hn LB LB	African Hymn (i)	Philip Harper	28
		African Hymn (ii)		30
B S B B	tpt hn hn LB	Waltzing Around (i)	Philip Harper	32
		Waltzing Around (ii)		34

*C = copper; B = bronze; S = silver
† tpt = trumpet, cornet or flugelhorn; hn = E flat horn or French horn; LB = trombone, baritone, euphonium or tuba.

Alternative versions
Horn parts are available in both E flat and F versions.
Parts for lower-brass instruments are available in both treble (B flat) and bass clef (C) versions.

Note for trombonists
Where appropriate, replace slurs with soft legato tonguing.
Occasionally, the trombone part is given as an ossia, in small type.

Duet   Soccarocca

John Miller

Duet Wonky Waltz

Nick Breeze

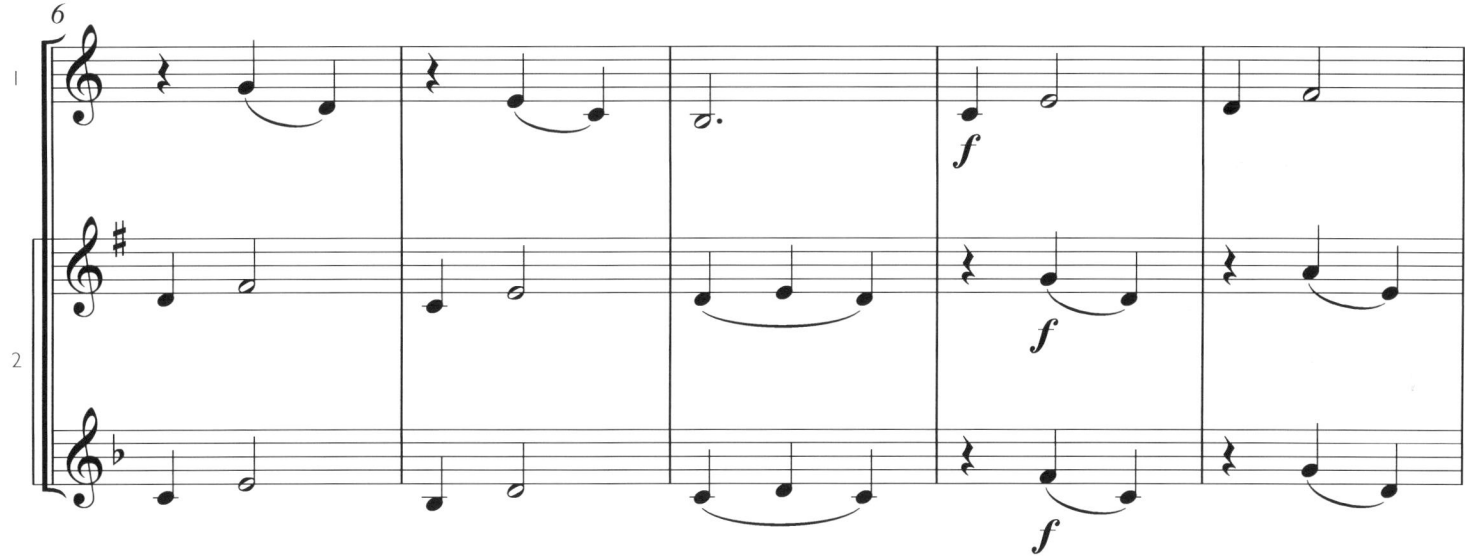

© 2006 by The Associated Board of the Royal Schools of Music

Duet   Megamarch

James Rae

Duet # Passing Through

Chris Batchelor

Duet   Two for Tea (i)

Philip Harper

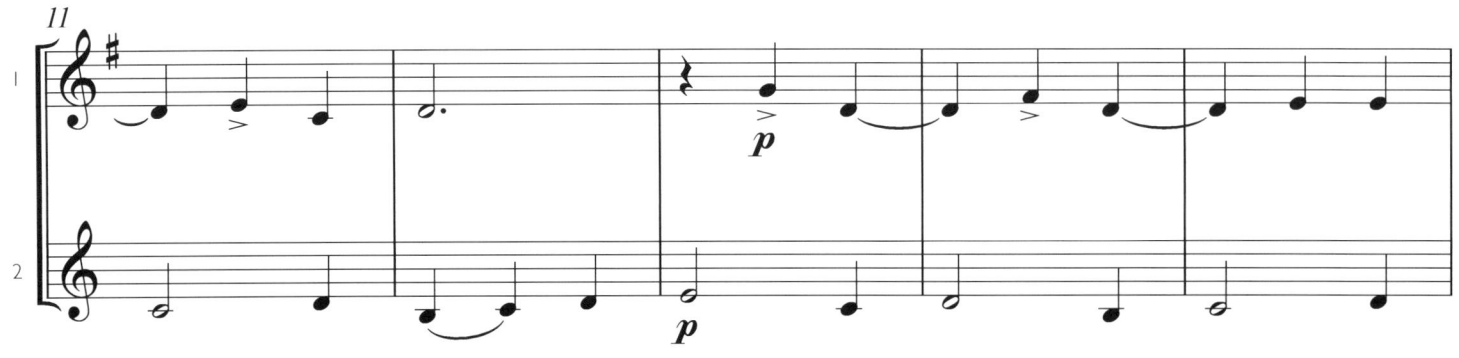

© 2006 by The Associated Board of the Royal Schools of Music

Duet   Two for Tea (ii)

Philip Harper

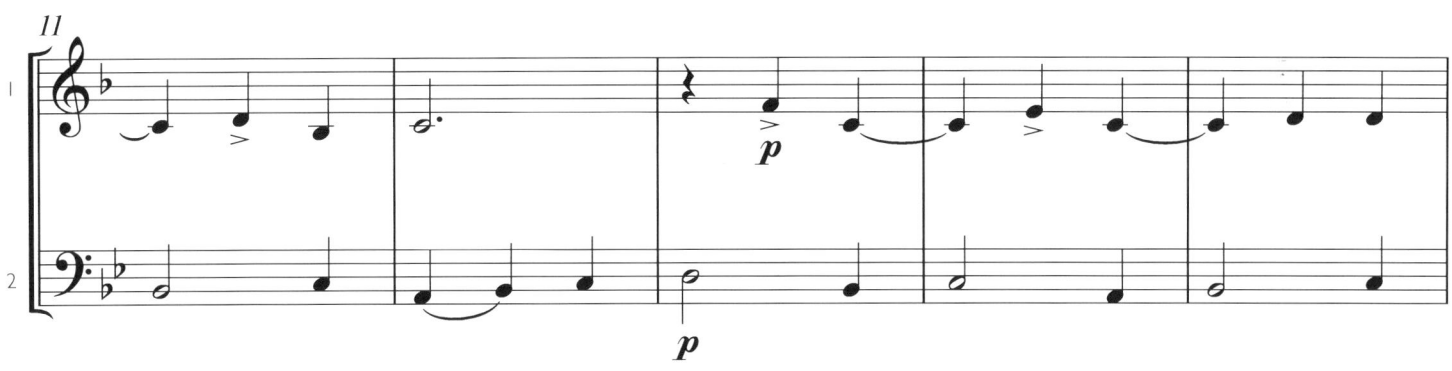

© 2006 by The Associated Board of the Royal Schools of Music

Duet   Bought me a cat (i)

Trad. American arr. Paul Archibald

Duet Bought me a cat (ii)

Trad. American arr. Paul Archibald

Brightly ♩ = *c.*112

Trio — Alpine Echo

Ian Lowes

Trio   Dancing Bears

Adrian Taylor

© 2006 by The Associated Board of the Royal Schools of Music

Trio — Promenade

Kit Turnbull

© 2006 by The Associated Board of the Royal Schools of Music

Tango para Tres (i)

Trio

Phil Croydon

Trio   Tango para Tres (ii)

Phil Croydon

Trio Russian Nights (i)

Philip Sparke

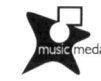

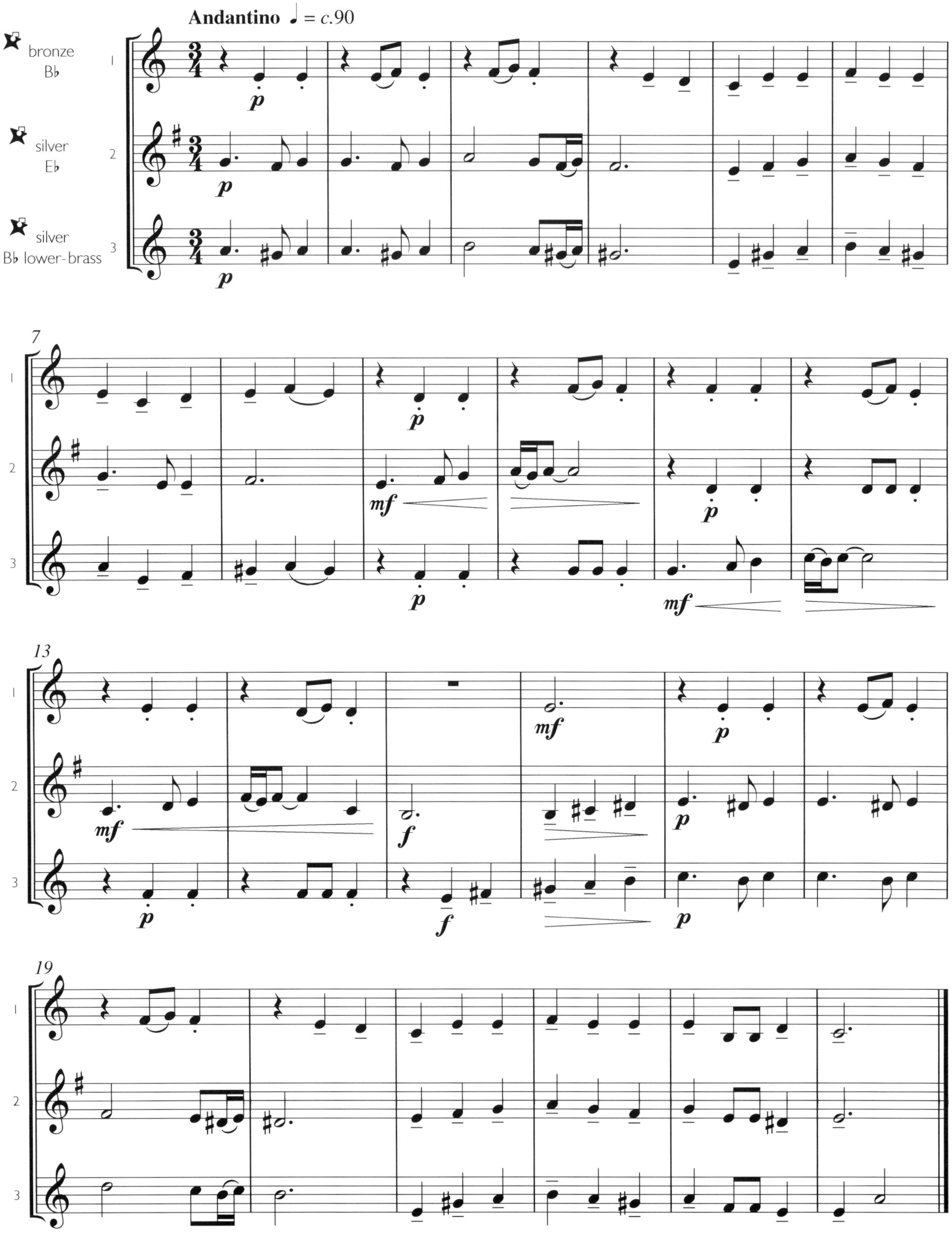

Used by kind permission of Anglo Music Press

Trio Russian Nights (ii)

Philip Sparke

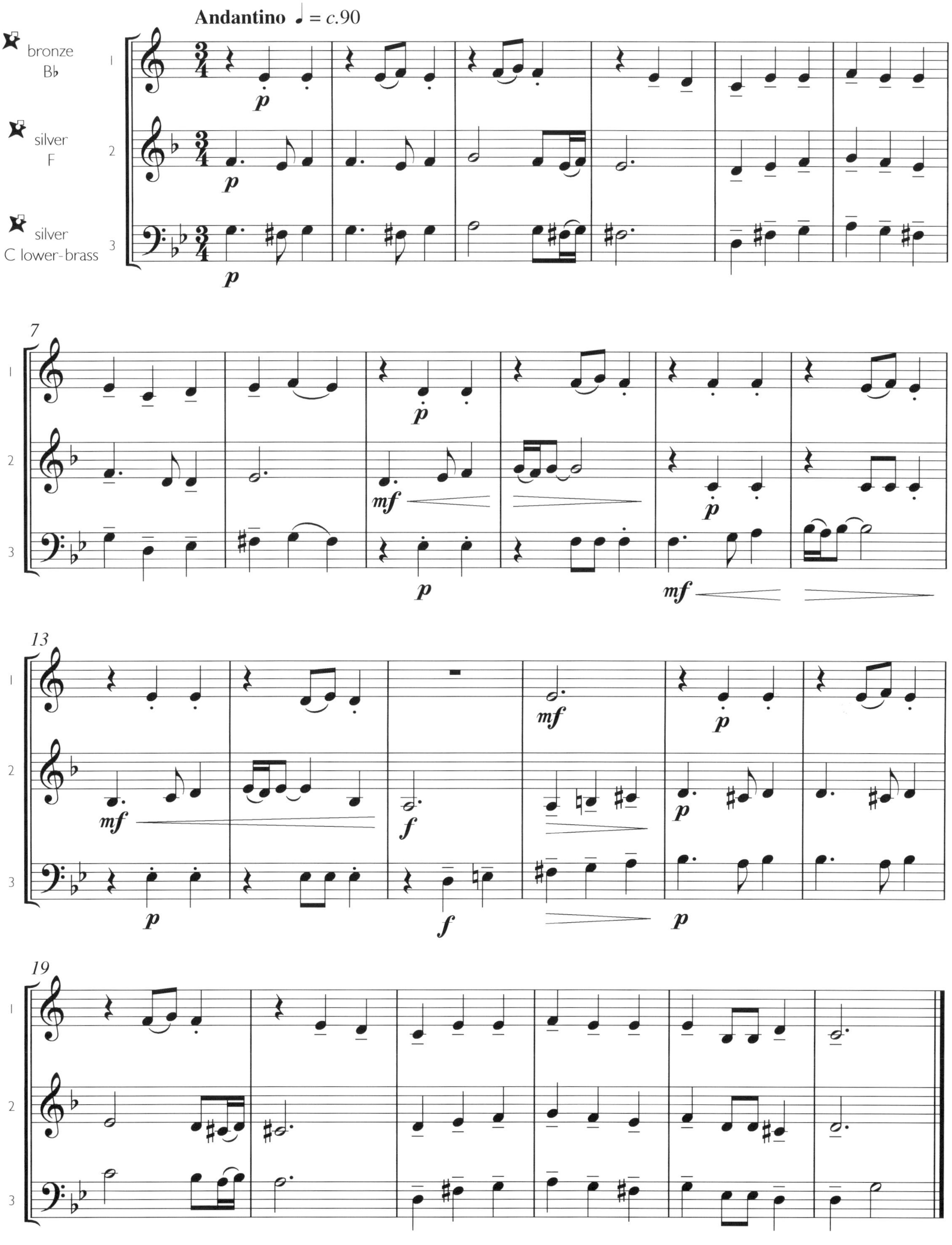

Used by kind permission of Anglo Music Press

Trio   Ye Kinge (i)

David Mitcham

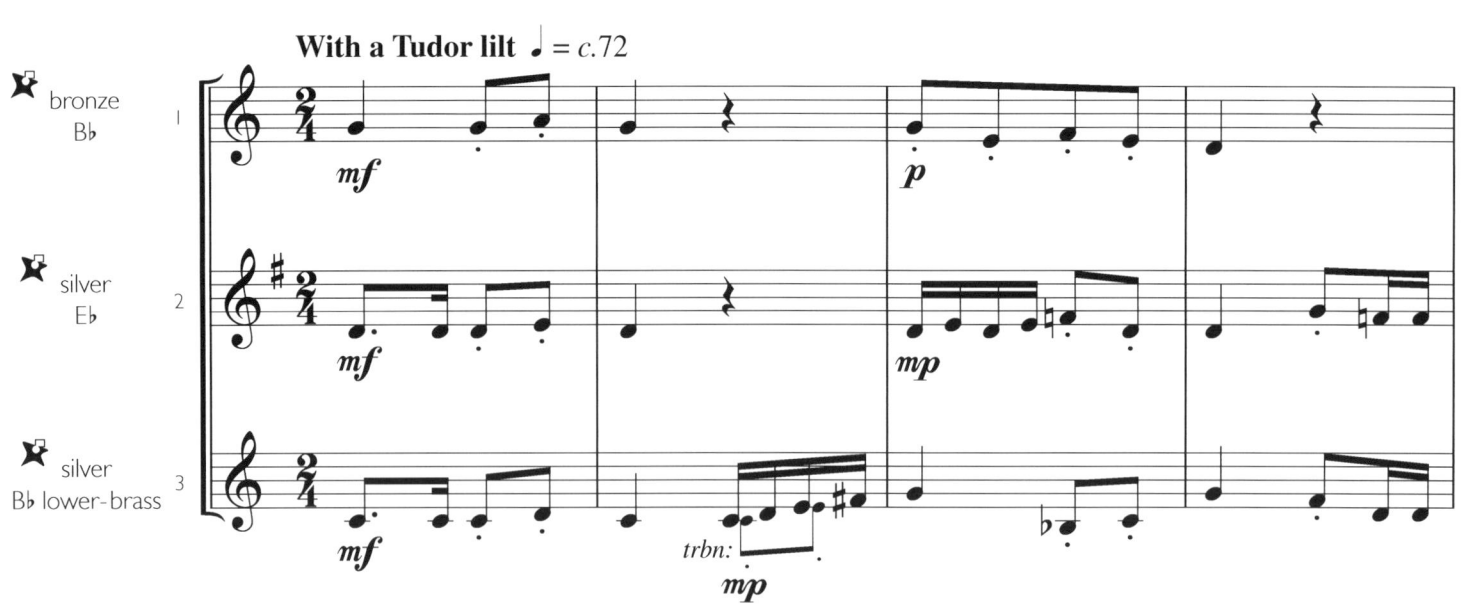
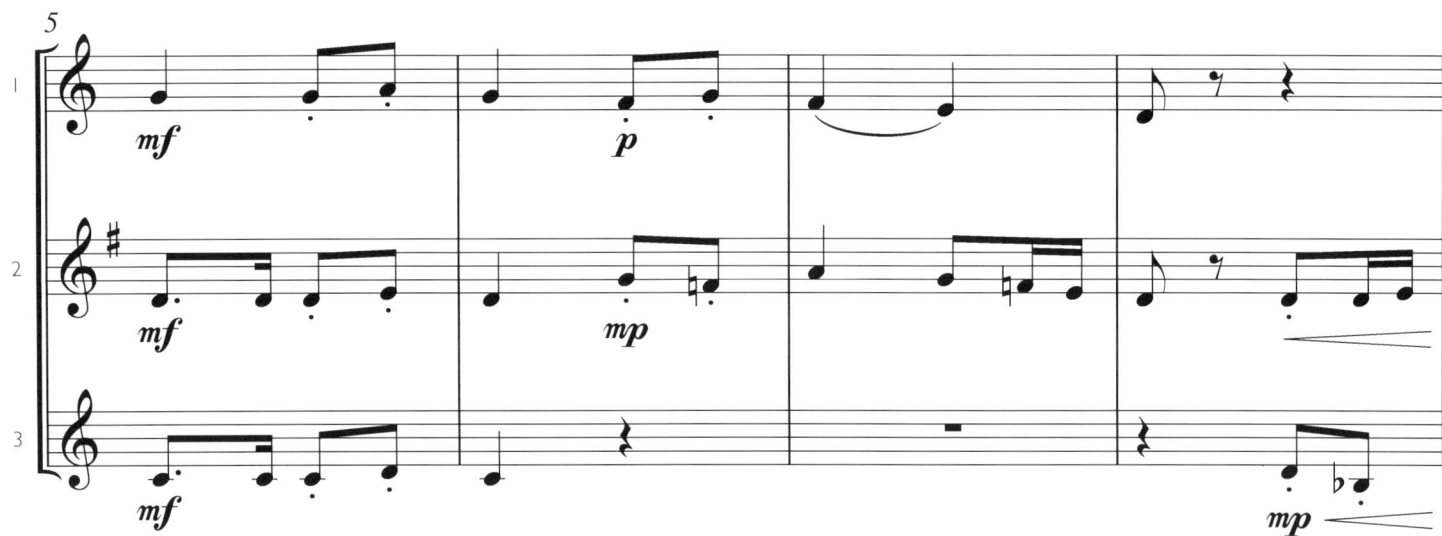

Trio   Ye Kinge (ii)

David Mitcham

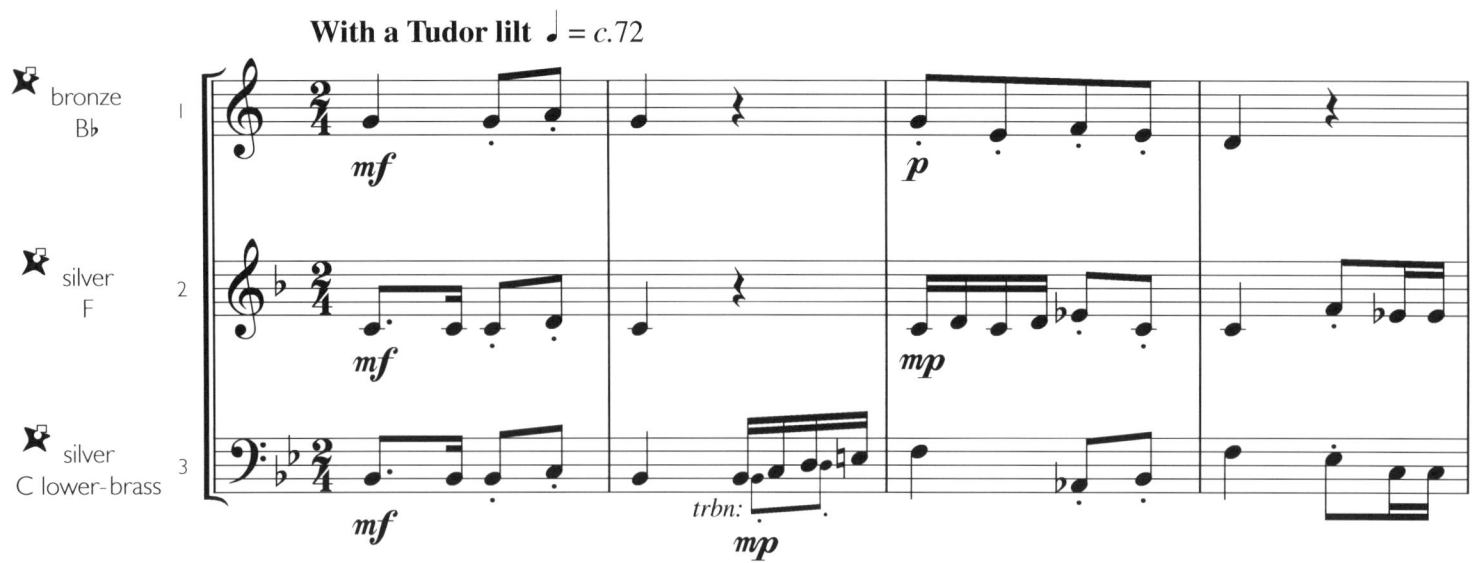

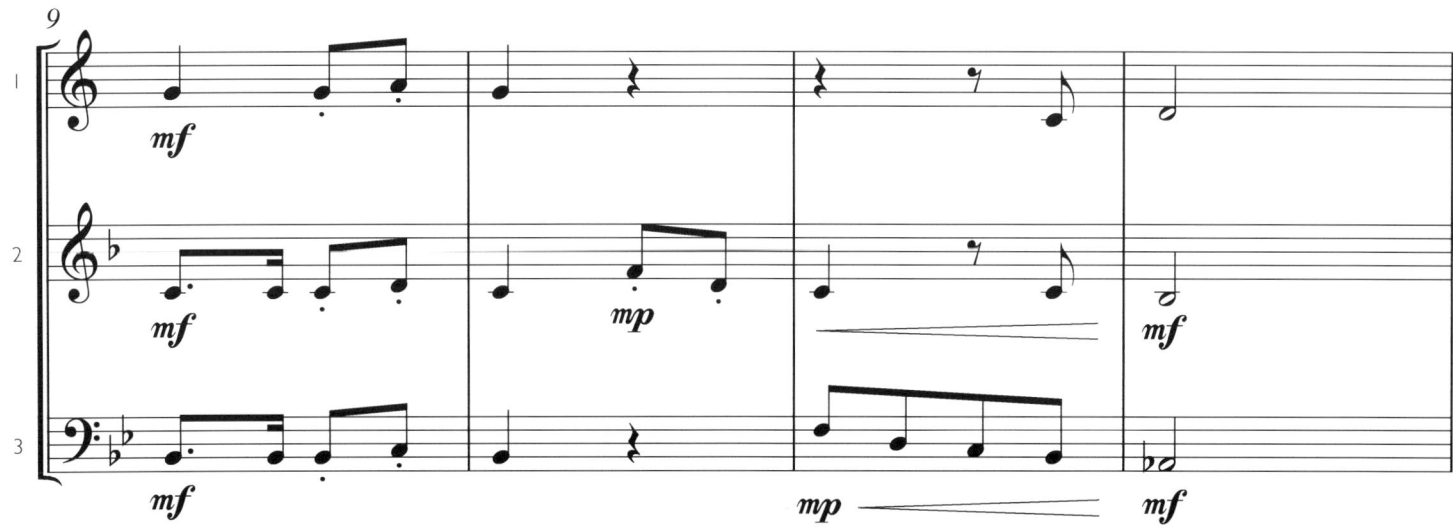

© 2006 by The Associated Board of the Royal Schools of Music

Trio   Country Dance (i)

Trad. arr. Paul Archibald

Trio — Country Dance (ii)

Trad. arr. Paul Archibald

Quartet March

Susato arr. Paul Archibald

© 2006 by The Associated Board of the Royal Schools of Music

Quartet Last Chance

Nick Breeze

© 2006 by The Associated Board of the Royal Schools of Music

Quartet African Hymn (i)

Philip Harper

Quartet African Hymn (ii)

Philip Harper

© 2006 by The Associated Board of the Royal Schools of Music

Quartet Waltzing Around (i)

Philip Harper

© 2006 by The Associated Board of the Royal Schools of Music

Quartet Waltzing Around (ii)

Philip Harper

© 2006 by The Associated Board of the Royal Schools of Music